MAGIC

URSULA SZWAST

Heinemann
LIBRARY

www.heinemann.co.uk/library
Visit our website to find out more information abou

To order:
☎ Phone 44 (0) 1865 888066
📄 Send a fax to 44 (0) 1865 314091
💻 Visit the Heinemann Bookshop at www.heinemann
catalogue and order online.

First published in Great Britain by Heinemann
Library, Halley Court, Jordan Hill, Oxford
OX2 8EJ, part of Harcourt Education.
Heinemann is a registered trademark of
Harcourt Education Ltd.

© Harcourt Education Ltd 2005
The moral right of the proprietor has been
asserted.

Editorial: Adam Miller and Kathy Peltan
Design: Joanna Turner
Picture Research: Stephanie Miller and
Jill Birschbach
Production: Camilla Smith

Originated by Ambassador Litho Ltd.
Printed China by WKT Company Ltd

The paper used to print this book comes from
sustainable resources

ISBN 0 431 11052 2
09 08 07 06 05
10 9 8 7 6 5 4 3 2 1

**British Library Cataloguing in Publication
Data**
Szwast, Ursula
   Magic. – (Get Going!. Hobbies)
   793.8

A full catalogue record for this book is available
from the British Library.

Acknowledgements
The Publishers would like to thank the following
for permission to reproduce photographs: p. 4
Syracuse Newspapers/The Image Works; pp. 5t,
10b, 13, 14, 15, 16, 17, 22, 23 Malcolm
Harris/Harcourteducation Ltd.; pp. 11, 18, 19,
20, 21, 24, 25, Robert Lifson/Heinemann Library;
pp. 5b, 7 Library of Congress; p. 6 Scala/Art
Resource, NY; p. 8 Nancy Sheehan/Photo Edit;
p. 9 plainpicture/Alamy; p. 10t Myrleen
Ferguson Cate/Photo Edit; pp. 12, 28 Jill
Birschbach/Heinemann Library; p. 27 Janet
Morgan/Heinemann Library; p. 29 Russell
Gordon.

Cover photograph of magician and assistant by
Royalty-free/Corbis.

The Publishers would like to thank Mr. Ash,
magician and owner of Ash's Magic Shop in
Chicago, for his comments that were used to
complete this book. Also, Peter Eldin, writer and
magician.

CONTENTS

What is magic? 4

A history of magic 6

Tips for performing magic tricks 8

Helpful equipment. 10

Card tricks. 12

Coin tricks. 18

Close-up magic 22

Magicians' organizations 28

Glossary 30

More books to read 31

Clubs, societies and websites 31

Index 32

Some words are shown in bold, **like this.** You can find out what they mean by looking in the glossary.

WHAT IS MAGIC?

You might have heard the expression "the hand is quicker than the eye". This expression refers to magic. People believe that magicians can do amazing tricks. They pull flowers out of a hat. They know what card a person is thinking about in a pack of cards. Sometimes they even make people "disappear".

This magician, Greg Steele, made it "snow" paper with a trick he performed at a school in New York.

Many people think that a magician's hand moves so quickly that the audience cannot follow the moves. The magician's hand, however, is not really quicker than the eye. What magicians do is carefully plan their moves and the words they use to **distract** the audience. They try to get the people in the audience to focus their attention to the wrong place at the right time. This is called **misdirection.**

KINDS OF MAGIC

Magicians perform different kinds of tricks. One kind of magic is called **sleight of hand.** To do these tricks, a magician has to learn skilful hand movements. Most sleight-of-hand tricks involve a pack of cards or some coins.

When performing close-up magic, the magician is close to the audience. Sometimes the people surround the magician as he or she performs the magic tricks, using cards, coins, or other small objects.

ILLUSION MAGIC

Illusion is a type of magic that involves large-scale tricks. The performer uses other people, animals, and large equipment. One of the most famous illusions has to do with sawing a person in half. Over the years, this illusion has been performed by several people. Other illusions involve making an object disappear or appear.

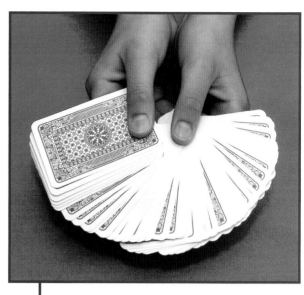

Get comfortable handling cards. There are many card tricks to master.

ESCAPE MAGIC

In escape magic, magicians put themselves in situations that appear to be impossible to get out of. For example, they may escape while being handcuffed and in leg irons.

MENTALIST MAGIC

Finally, some magicians perform a type of magic called mentalist magic. These magicians claim to be able to read people's minds and predict events. One mentalist claimed to have read the mind of a person who was underwater in a submarine.

As you can see, magicians perform a variety of amazing tricks. This book will show you how to entertain people using mostly sleight-of-hand and close-up magic tricks.

The magician Harry Houdini performed daring escapes in films and for live audiences.

A HISTORY OF MAGIC

MAGIC IN ANCIENT TIMES

Magic has entertained people throughout history. One of the oldest known **sleight-of-hand** tricks, known as the cups and balls trick, was performed in ancient Egypt in about 2500 BC. The trick was also performed in ancient Greece and Rome.

Records from the first century AD show that magicians in ancient times also performed **illusion** magic. One report describes the doors of a temple opening when fires were lit. Another report describes trumpets that sounded without people playing them. Ancient Egyptians, Greeks, and Romans also saw magicians perform at various festivals.

MAGIC IN THE MIDDLE AGES

Magicians continued to entertain people into the **Middle Ages.** In the 1300s, a traveller known as Ibn Batuta wrote about a magic trick he saw in the palace of a Chinese ruler. Ibn Batuta wrote about a juggler who threw a long strap into the air. The juggler then commanded a boy to climb the strap, which he did. This illusion, known as the Indian rope trick, has been reported in other places of the world throughout history.

Hieronymus Bosch made this painting in about 1475. It shows a magician performing a trick.

By the 1500s, magicians throughout Europe entertained people with card tricks and by making all kinds of objects disappear. One magician was named Boccal. Accounts of Boccal's magic describe a trick in which he asked for a bottle of wine and popped the cork. He emptied the bottle and threw the cork into a nearby pool of water. The cork later reappeared on a string around the neck of an audience member!

MODERN MAGIC

John Henry Anderson, from Scotland, performed his magic tricks throughout the United States and other countries in the mid-1800s. One of the tricks he is best remembered for is appearing to catch a bullet from a gun fired by a member of the audience.

In the mid-1800s, the famous French magician Jean-Eugène Robert-Houdin entertained audiences with his illusion tricks. Robert-Houdin is thought to be the first great modern illusionist. He became known as the father of modern magic. He also inspired Eric Weisz, who is better known by his stage name – Harry Houdini.

FAMOUS MAGICIANS

Harry Houdini was a famous American escape magician. He seemed to be able to free himself from seemingly inescapable situations. His fame as an escape artist spread throughout the world. By 1900, crowds filled his shows in theatres everywhere. One of Houdini's most astonishing tricks, the Chinese water torture escape, involved him escaping from an airtight tank filled with water.

Today, the magician David Copperfield is famous for both his sleight-of-hand tricks and for his illusion stunts. He performs hundreds of live shows throughout the world as well as on television. He is famous for spectacular outdoor illusion tricks. In one trick he made New York's famous Statue of Liberty "disappear".

This poster advertised a trick in which Houdini was going to escape from being buried alive in a coffin. He died in 1926 before he could perform the trick.

TIPS FOR PERFORMING MAGIC TRICKS

Performing magic tricks for an audience can be a lot of fun. You do not need a special place to perform. A living room, classroom, or theatre stage are all good places for you to show your talents.

PREPARING YOUR ACT

Before you host a magic show, you need to know how to perform several magic tricks. But the number of tricks you know is not as important as how well you perform them. It is better to perform just a few tricks well rather than many tricks poorly.

Of course, to become a good magician, you have to practise your tricks. The more you practise, the better you will be. Your aim is to make your tricks as **deceptive** as possible. Getting the **timing** right will help you do this. Setting up a **patter** will also help. When you perform a magic trick, what you say is just as important as what you do. It becomes part of the **misdirection** required to fool your audience.

Once you master a few tricks, you could perform a short magic show for your friends or classmates.

It is a good idea to write down what you want to say while performing your tricks. Then memorize it and use it during your act.

A good way to improve your tricks is to practise them in front of a mirror. You could also video yourself and then watch the video to see which parts of your act need improvement.

KEEPING YOUR AUDIENCE'S ATTENTION

When performing your magic, your main task is to keep your audience's attention. It is important to use misdirection to **distract** the people in the audience so they do not notice what you are really doing. A good magician never performs a magic trick without practising it until it can be presented without hesitation. To grab the audience's attention, start out with a simple, yet eye-catching, trick. Use your longer tricks in the middle of your act. Then finish the act with your most amazing trick.

You will be able to keep up the deception by following some simple rules that all magicians follow. First, never tell your audience how to do a trick. Second, do not do the same trick more than once in a performance. Doing it more than once might allow the audience to work out how you did the trick.

This young magician made a hat hover in mid-air!

HELPFUL EQUIPMENT

To make your act even more **impressive**, you could wear a costume. The kind of costume you create is up to you. A magician's waistcoat, cape, or top hat can help you look the part.

You will need a few pieces of equipment to perform many of your magic tricks. You will probably find most of the things you need in your own home.

CARDS

Many **sleight-of-hand** tricks use playing cards, so a pack of cards is an important part of your equipment. Have several complete packs available.

*This boy chose a **traditional** magician's hat and cape to complete his costume.*

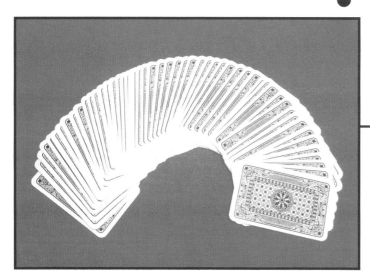

There are 52 cards in a full pack.

MAGIC WAND

A wand adds a special touch to your magic tricks. You can buy a wand, or make one and decorate it. A scarf or a large handkerchief can help create the **deception** you need in some of your tricks.

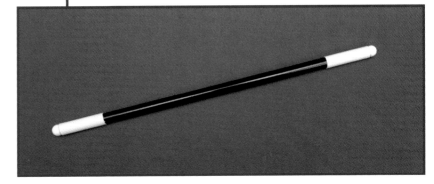

You can buy a wand like this, or make your own using a stick or cardboard.

CUPS AND BALLS

Cups and balls were used in one of the earliest known magic tricks. These can be helpful in performing several different magic tricks.

You can use ordinary plastic cups and buy some rubber balls to perform cups and balls tricks.

COINS

Coins are also used in many magic tricks. You can use coins you already have or ask for **volunteers** from the audience to contribute coins.

Ten-pence pieces or US quarters are a good size for sleight-of-hand tricks.

CARD TRICKS

Some of the most popular magic tricks are card tricks. Here are some tricks that you can add to your magic act.

THE ABRACADABRA TRICK

You will need:
21 cards, chosen at **random** from a full pack of cards

1 Deal the 21 cards, face up, into 3 **columns** by dealing 7 **rows** of 3. Deal the cards, starting at your left and dealing to the right. The photo on this page shows how the cards should look.

2 As you deal the cards, tell the audience what you are doing.

3 Choose someone from the audience and tell him or her to think of any card in one of the columns. Tell the **volunteer** to remember the chosen card, but not tell you what it is.

4 Ask the person to tell you which column the card is in.

5 Pick up the cards in one of the columns, then the column that the volunteer's card is in, and then the last column. You must pick up the cards one card at a time starting at either the top or the bottom of each column. The cards should remain face up until step 14. Place each new card at the bottom of the pile in your hand. The column of cards that has the chosen card should be between the other two columns of cards.

6 Deal the cards out again, just as you did in step 1.

7 Ask the same person from the audience to tell you which column the card is in this time.

8 Repeat step 5.

9 Deal the cards a third time, and ask the audience member to tell you which column the card is in now.

10 Repeat step 5.

11 Now it's time to find the card.

12 Hold the cards face down in your hand. Ask the volunteer if he or she has ever heard the word ABRACADABRA.

13 Tell the audience that ABRACADABRA is a magic word that you will use to find the card. Flip the pile of cards over in your hand and hold the cards face down.

14 Spell ABRACADABRA out loud and deal one card for each letter in the word. Deal the cards face down, starting from the top of the pile. When you get to the last A of the magic word, turn over that card. That card will be the chosen card.

THE FOUR ACES TRICK

You will need:
a pack of cards

1 Before you start your trick, place four aces, face down, on top of the pack.

2 Place the pack of cards on the table. Ask a **volunteer** to **cut** the pack into four piles.

3 While the volunteer is cutting the pack, be aware of which pile has the aces.

4 Pick up one pile, but not the pile with the aces. That pile should be picked up last. Take three cards from the top of the pile that you picked up and place them on the bottom of the pile.

5 Then take three cards from the top of this pile. Place one card on top of each of the other three piles.

6 Repeat steps 4 and 5 with the other three piles. Handle the pile with the aces last.

7 When you have finished handling all four piles, ask a volunteer to turn over the top card of each pile.

8 The volunteer should find that all four cards are aces!

ANOTHER GREAT CARD TRICK

You will need:
a pack of cards

1 Look at the bottom card of the pack before you start this trick. You have to remember this card.

2 Ask a **volunteer** to **cut**, or separate, the pack into five piles.

3 Ask him or her to choose the top card of one of the piles, look at it, and remember that card.

4 Pick up all five piles of cards. Make sure you place the pile with the bottom card that you remembered on top of the pile that has the card that the volunteer chose. That will place the volunteer's card immediately next to your memorized card.

5 If the volunteer chooses the top card of the pile that has the card you remembered, tell the volunteer to cut the pile. Then complete the cut, placing the part of the pile with your memorized card on top of the other part.

6 Then put the other piles together in any order.

7 Now tell the audience that you will find the card the volunteer chose.

8 Hold the pack of cards face down in your hand. Starting with the top card, place each card face up until you find your memorized card. The next card that you place face up will be the card the volunteer chose.

9 Point to that card as proof of your magical powers.

Don't forget the card that you memorize. It is the key to knowing which card your volunteer picked.

COIN TRICKS

SWITCH THE COIN TRICK

You will need:
two coins

1 Ask a **volunteer** in the audience for two coins. If no one offers, provide two coins of your own.

2 Place a coin in the palm of each hand. Place the coin in your left hand just below the fingers, near your thumb.

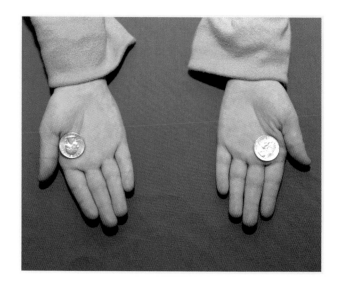

3 Place the other coin in your right hand near your thumb. Show your palms to the audience.

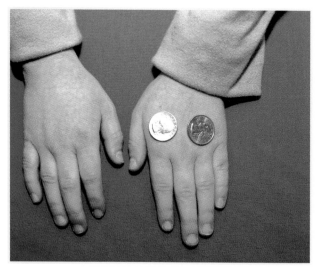

The purpose of the above photo is to show that both coins should be under your left hand after you complete step 4.

4 The next step has to be done quickly and precisely. At exactly the same time, quickly turn both hands over, so the thumbs come close together. As you make this move, toss the coin in your right hand under the left hand.

5 If you do this correctly, the people in the audience will think that you only turned your hands over. They will expect to see a coin under each hand.

6 Lift your right hand. Tell the audience that your magic has made the coin disappear from under your right hand.

7 Then lift your left hand. Tell the audience that your amazing powers have made an extra coin appear under your left hand.

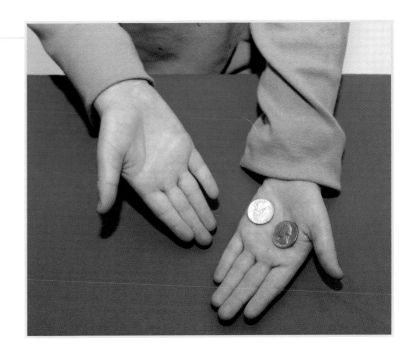

THE KING OF COINS

Coin tricks have been performed for hundreds of years. One performer, T. Nelson Downs, became known as the King of Coins because he specialized in coin tricks and amazed audiences with them. Two of his books are considered excellent guides to help magicians master **sleight-of-hand** magic.

In 1900, he published a book called *Modern Coin Manipulation.* In the book he revealed how to perform several of his famous coin tricks. One trick called "The **Miser's** Dream" resulted in a shower of coins being rained down upon the magician. He published *The Art of Magic* in 1921.

COIN IN POCKET TRICK

You will need:
a coin
a large handkerchief
a shirt or jacket with a breast pocket

1 Hold a coin between the thumb and index finger of your left hand. Keep your hand chest-high, and 45 centimetres in front of your body.

2 Hold the handkerchief in your right hand and cover the coin.

3 Pull the handkerchief towards your body so that your right hand rests evenly with the pocket on your shirt or jacket.

4 Keep pulling the handkerchief so that the audience can see the coin again.

5 Now repeat steps 1 to 3. But this time, when your right hand meets your left hand, grab the coin between your right index finger and thumb. Keep moving the handkerchief toward you, but be **deceptive** and do not let the audience see what you are doing. Keep the coin covered with the handkerchief at this point.

6 Keep moving your right hand and the coin covered by the handkerchief towards your pocket.

7 When your hand gets near your pocket, let the coin drop into it.

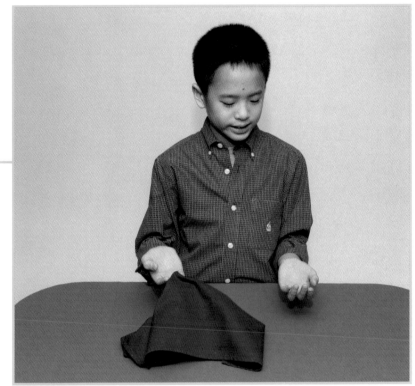

8 Keep moving the handkerchief over the left hand and show that the coin has disappeared!

9 Show your audience that both of your hands are empty. Tell them to check the empty handkerchief.

TRICK TIPS

1. Practise all your tricks in front of a mirror so you see your tricks in the same way the audience does. Practise as much as you can.
2. Practise your **patter**, or what you will say during your performance.
3. Try not to tell how tricks work. The audience will be more **impressed**.
4. Borrow items from the audience to use in your tricks. This reassures the audience that you have not done anything to the items before the show.

CLOSE-UP MAGIC

PAPER CLIP TRICK

You will need:
a £5 note
two paper clips

1 Show the audience a stretched-out £5 note.

2 Fold the left third of the £5 note to the right. Place a paper clip from the top of the note over this part to hold it in place, as shown in the photo. The clip should be placed exactly as it is in this photo.

3 Turn the note over so that you are looking at the other side and the clip is at the top. Do not turn the note upside down.

4 Fold the left end of the note over to the right towards the folded part.

5 Place a paper clip on the £5 note from the top. Only clip together the two front folds of the note. Again, the clip should be placed exactly as shown in the photo on the right.

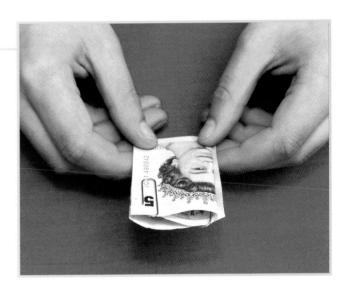

6 Now tightly hold the ends of the £5 note as shown in the photo. Start pulling the ends apart.

7 When the clips are almost next to each other, sharply pull apart the ends of the note. The paper clips will shoot toward you and they will be linked together.

8 Point out your magic powers to the audience!

KNOT TRICK

You will need:
a piece of thin rope 1 metre long
a piece of magician's wax
or a small piece of white glue stick

1 Before you start, stick a small piece of the wax or glue stick about two-thirds of the way down the rope. The audience should not see you do this.

2 Hold the rope outstretched with both hands. The part with the wax or glue should be facing you.

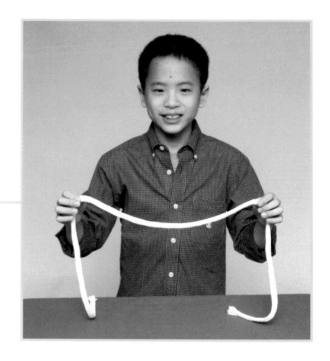

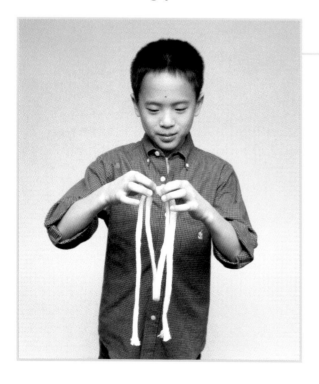

3 Keep your right hand still while you move the rope with your left hand to the right. Stick a piece of rope on the wax or glue. Press the rope hard with your right thumb to keep it in place.

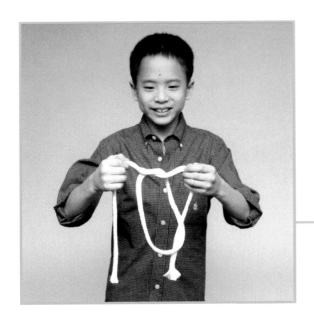

4 Use the middle finger of your left hand to pull the piece of rope that is hanging through the loop. This should look as if you have made a knot. Hold this out for the audience to see.

5 Tell the audience that you will now perform the magic.

6 Move both wrists outwards and the rope will fly up. The "knot" will have disappeared.

7 Point out your magical skills to everyone in the audience.

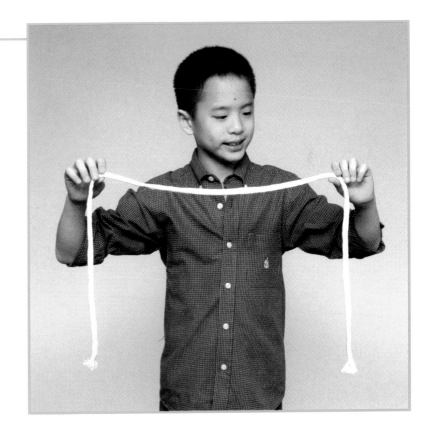

CUPS AND BALLS TRICK

You will need:
three paper or plastic cups
two paper, rubber, or plastic balls (You can make the balls from tissue paper, but it is important that they are all the same size.)
a magic wand

1 Hide one ball inside one of the cups. Stack all three cups so that the one with the hidden ball is in the middle. Place the stack of cups on the table.

2 Put the remaining ball on the table, beside the stack of cups.

3 Pick up the cups, with the mouths facing upwards. Remove the cup closest to you and point the cup slightly towards the audience. Do not let the people see completely inside the cup. Then place the cup mouth down on the table. Move smoothly when you do this.

4 Remove the next cup, and point it slightly away from the audience, so that they do not see the ball that you placed inside. Turn this cup, mouth down, on the table to the right of the first cup. The ball you hid will now be under this cup. Make sure your moves look the same this time as they did when you pulled off the first cup.

5 Take the last cup and point it slightly towards the audience, using the same smooth movements you used with the two other cups. Place the cup mouth down, to the right of the other two cups.

6 Pick up the ball that is on the table. Place it on top of the cup that is in the centre.

7 Ask the people in the audience where the ball is. They should tell you it is on top of the centre cup.

8 Tell them that you will use your magic powers and show them that the ball is not on the top of the cup but underneath it.

9 Place the cup on your right on top of the ball on the centre cup (that also contains the hidden ball). Then place the cup on the left on top of these cups. Take your magic wand and tap the stack of cups.

10 Then lift up the stack of three cups to show that there is a ball under the bottom cup. Tell the audience that your magic power has pushed the ball through to the inside of the cup!

There are specialist magic shops, like this one, in many US cities.

There are many ways that you can learn more about doing magic tricks. One way is by finding information in books about magic tricks. You can also join one of the national magic organizations, or a local magic club. They will help you to make your performance more interesting and fun, and also how to find equipment for your show.

THE MAGIC CIRCLE

The Magic Circle is one of the most important magic organizations in the world. It was formed in London in 1905 by a group of 23 magicians, but there are now about 1500 members in 38 countries, dedicated to promoting the art of magic. Many of its members are world-famous **professional** magicians. Some are Members of the Inner Magic Circle, a special honour only awarded to a few magicians each year.

In 1998 this 100-year-old organization opened its own purpose-built headquarters near London's West End. There is a theatre that hosts regular shows open to the public, as well as special events, such as the Magician of the Year awards. The library has the largest collection of magic books in Europe, and the museum contains fascinating posters and items associated with magic through the ages.

BRITISH MAGICAL SOCIETY

This society is based in Birmingham and was founded a few months before the Magic Circle. Many of its members belong to both societies. The British Magical Society has a library of nearly 2000 books available on loan to its members, and a free newsletter. Its members also produce *Abracadabra,* the international magazine about magic.

SOCIETY OF AMERICAN MAGICIANS

Formed in 1902, this is the oldest organization for magic in the world. It has more than 7000 members, as well as its Society of Young Magicians which has 1000 members aged seven to fifteen.

INTERNATIONAL BROTHERHOOD OF MAGICIANS

This is the world's largest organization for magicians. Started in 1922, it now has more than 14,000 members, both **amateur** and **professional** magicians.

MAGIC CLUBS FOR YOUNG PEOPLE

The Magic Circle's Young Magician's Club helps young people aged 10 to 18 become the fine magicians of the future. The club has its own magazine, *Secrets,* and organizes competitions and hands-on workshops for members. The British Magical Society has a junior section for ages 10 to 16 that meets every two weeks on Saturday mornings, in Birmingham.

There are also Magic Clubs in many cities throughout the UK. Many clubs organize exciting demonstrations by professional magicians, or arrange for people who sell supplies for magicians to come and display them at the club. All these clubs and organizations can help you to become a better performer.

After a few years of practice, you could put on your own shows like this magician.

GLOSSARY

amateur   person who does something for enjoyment rather than for money

column   vertical, or up-and-down, arrangement of items

cut   divide a pack of playing cards by lifting a section from the top of the pile

deceptive   meant to mislead

distract   to draw the attention away from something

illusion   type of magic that involves presenting misleading images or events

impressive   having the power to impress, or move or affect people strongly

Middle Ages   time in British and European history from about 500 to about 1450

misdirection   process of focusing audience attention to a place or spot that hides what the magician is actually doing

miser   person who lives poorly in order to save and store money

patter   talk that entertainers use while performing routines

professional   person who takes part in an activity for money rather than for fun

random   in no particular order

row   series of things arranged in a horizontal, or side-to-side, line

sleight-of-hand   type of magic that involves using skilful hand movements

timing   ability to select the precise moment for doing something in order to achieve maximum effect

tradition   handing down of beliefs, customs, or information from one generation to the next

volunteer   person who willingly offers to do something

MORE BOOKS TO READ

Baddiel, Ivor; Zucker, Jonny et al, *Mystical Magic* (Scholastic Hippo, 2003)

Bull, Jane, *The Magic Book* (Dorling Kindersley, 2002)

Eldin, Peter, *Magic with Cards,* (Aladdin Books, 2002)

Eldin, Peter, *Mind Magic* (Aladdin Books, 2002)

Ho, Oliver, *Magic Tricks (Young Magicians series),*
    (Sterling Juvenile Books, 2003)

Presto, Fay, *Magic Tricks* (Kingfisher, 2002).

CLUBS, SOCIETIES AND WEBSITES

The Magic Circle
Centre for the Magic Arts
12 Stephenson Way
London, NW1 2HD
www.themagiccircle.co.uk

This is the junior branch of the Magic Circle
The Young Magicians Club
www.theyoungmagiciansclub.com

The British Magical Society
(Senior and Junior sections)
The Selly Oak Ex-Servicemens' Club
8 Selly Hill Road
Selly Oak, Birmingham
B29 7DL
www.britishmagicalsociety.co.uk

www.ukmagic.net/clubs.htm
lists local UK magic clubs

www.kidzone.ws/magic/index.htm
this site has instructions for some magic tricks to try at home

www.magicians.org.au
site for the Australian Society of Magicians

INDEX

abracadabra trick 12–13
ancient time, magic in 6
Anderson, John Henry 7
audience 4, 9, 11, 21

Boccal 6
books about magic 19, 28, 31
borrowing items from the audience 21
British Magical Society 28, 31
bullets, catching 7

card tricks 5, 6, 12–17
  abracadabra trick 12–13
  four aces trick 14–15
  naming the card trick 16–17
cards, pack of 4, 10
close-up magic 4, 22–7
  cups and balls trick 6, 26–7
  knot trick 24–5
  paper clip trick 22–3
clubs for magicians 28-31
coin tricks 18–21
  coin in pocket trick 20–1
  switch the coin trick 18–19
coins 4, 11
Copperfield, David 7
costume 10
cups and balls 11
cups and balls trick 6, 26–7

deception 8, 9, 11
distraction 4, 9
Downs, T. Nelson 19

Egypt, ancient 6
equipment 10–11, 29
  cards 4, 10
  coins 4, 11
  costume 10
  cups and balls 11
  handkerchiefs and scarves 11, 20–1
  wand 11
escape magic 5, 7

four aces trick 14–15

Greece, ancient 6

hand movements 4
  see also sleight-of-hand tricks
handkerchiefs and scarves 11, 20–1
history of magic 6–7
Houdini, Harry 5, 7
Houdini Museum 31

Ibn Batuta 6
illusion magic 5, 6, 7
Indian rope trick 6
International Brotherhood of Magicians 29, 31

knot trick 24–5

magazines 29
Magic Circle 28, 31
Magic clubs 29, 31
Member of the Inner Circle 29
mentalist magic 5
Middle Ages 6
misdirection 4, 8, 9

naming the card trick 16–17

organizations 28–9

paper clip trick 22–3
patter 8, 21
practice 8, 9, 21
preparing your act 8–9
professional magicians 28–9

Robert-Houdin, Jean-Eugène 7
Romans 6
rope
  Indian rope trick 6
  knot trick 24–5

sawing a person in half 5
sleight-of-hand tricks 4, 6, 7, 10, 19
Society of American Magicians 29
Society of Young Magicians 29
specialist stores 4, 28
Steele, Greg 4
switch the coin trick 18–19

timing 8

wand 11

young magicians 28, 29
Young Magicians Club 29, 31

Titles in the *Get Going: Hobbies* series include:

Hardback   0 431 11050 6

Hardback   0 431 11051 4

Hardback   0 431 11052 2

Find out about the other titles in this series on our website www.heinemann.co.uk/library